SQUARE HOLE
FOR A
SQUARE PEG

SQUARE HOLE
FOR A
SQUARE PEG
Second Edition

EXONA MOLL

Square Hole for a Square Peg

Copyright © 2022 by Exona Moll. All rights reserved.

No part of this publication may be reproduced, stored in a retrieval system or transmitted in any way by any means, electronic, mechanical, photocopy, recording or otherwise without the prior permission of the author except as provided by USA copyright law.

The opinions expressed by the author are not necessarily those of URLink Print and Media.

Page 36 map - copyrighted property of Waterways World Ltd. 151 Station Street, Burton-on-Trent. Staffs. DE14 1BG.

1603 Capitol Ave., Suite 310 Cheyenne, Wyoming USA 82001
1-888-980-6523 | admin@urlinkpublishing.com

URLink Print and Media is committed to excellence in the publishing industry.

Book design copyright © 2022 by URLink Print and Media. All rights reserved.

Published in the United States of America

Library of Congress Control Number: 2022911909
ISBN 978-1-68486-218-4 (Paperback)
ISBN 978-1-68486-219-1 (Digital)

26.05.22

CONTENTS

Part I

Chapter 1: Forming the Peg 9

Chapter 2: The World's Round Hole 10

Chapter 3: Life Begins to Unravel 12

Chapter 4: Life Fell Off a Cliff 15

Chapter 5: Picking Up the Pieces 17

Chapter 6: Starting on the Square Hole 19

Chapter 7: The Secret Life of Zona 22

Chapter 8: Life Restarted 24

Part II

Chapter 1: Life on a Boat 33

Chapter 2: Life as I Intended It to Be 35

Chapter 3: The Winter Routine 37

Chapter 4: Summers As I Originally Intended 39

Chapter 5: Winter Really Wild 44

Chapter 6: My Second Summer 47

Chapter 7: A Rather Different Winter 49

PART I

CHAPTER 1

Forming the Peg

I was born in Oxford during the Second World War. We lived in a suburb of Oxford where there were all large houses and mostly elderly folks. We lived in a flat that was the upstairs in my grandmother's house. Grandma was an invalid, and I was not to disturb her.

I started school at the local infants' school, but I was always sick. So my parents sent me as a day girl to a nearby boarding school. It was a good start for me; I learnt all about good speech, good grammar, and the importance of keeping one's arms in at mealtimes, etc. But we day girls were always outsiders.

When I was nine, my brother was born. Six months later, we moved to a council house on an estate on the other side of Oxford, and I changed to a state school.

I was teased a lot, as I spoke differently from the other kids at school. I did not want to lose my Queen's English, but after a little while (and for selfpreservation), I copied the other kids at school. At home, though, I kept my good accent. For many years, I was able to turn my Queen's English on and off as I wished.

CHAPTER
2

The World's Round Hole

When it came to leaving school, I did not fancy any of the jobs that were on offer for girls. When the time actually came, I still had not found a job. My mother suggested I follow in her footsteps and try for a post as a GPO telephonist. I took her advice and got a job in Oxford Telephone Exchange. It was a good job, one I quite enjoyed. I did not like being inside all the time, where I could not even see the daylight. One aspect I did like, though, was the chance to do relief work at other exchanges.

At one point, I went to the employment exchange. They had no outdoor jobs for girls, not even something that would involve travelling about.

By now, most of my workmates were dating boys, but I had no interest in boys at all. I found that one thing I did like was dancing. I went most Saturday nights to the local dance hall. Soon, the inevitable happened: I met a boy who was a great dancer.

By then I had a motor scooter, and he had a motorbike. He also helped me with my scooter. I found that unlike the boys at school, he neither teased me nor looked down on me for being a girl. We started courting, and after some time, he proposed. My problem was that while I did not want to get married, I also did not want to lose him.

To add to the complication, I had just found the job I was looking for. When I was accepted to the Women's Royal Naval Service (or

WRNS), it was the first real crossroads in my life. Do I take the risk of joining up? Do I do the thing most girls did—get married and have children? Though I had always been close to my mum, for the first time in my life, I felt I could not discuss this with her.

I was very fond of Alan; I could not bring myself to finish with him. I thought I loved him enough, so I turned the WRNS down, and we got married.

Being a wife and a homemaker did not come easily to me. We could not afford a house in Oxford, so we bought a house in Witney, which was a mistake. The house needed modernising, and the builder said it was a six-month job. Believing him was another mistake. By the time it was done, eighteen months later, I was a nervous wreck.

CHAPTER

3

Life Begins to Unravel

Alan had always said he wanted children. When at last the building was finished, I said, "If we are going to try for a family, we had better get on with it". I was pregnant within two months. Nine months later my son was born. Fifteen months after that my daughter was born. I had always said, "If I have children at all, I will have more than one and have them close together".

Being a mother did not come any more naturally to me than being a wife. It was all beginning to get too much for me. I began the slow decent into the slough of despair.

I was struggling through various levels of depression. (But depression was not taken seriously in those days). Life was becoming more of a fog. Every so often I would have a crisis, that I called 'a crash'. Each time that happened I lost another chunk of my memory.

My memories of that period are just odd snatches:

> Scared of feeling happy because I knew a deeper low would follow

> Worse was the sleep; or rather the lack of it. I never seemed to sleep deeply enough to get any benefit from it. I would wake in the morning feeling more tired than when I went to bed

> On one occasioin, there were two voices in my head; one good and one evil, having a battle, I was just listening.

> The cycling helped, as long as the children did not play up. As exercise flushed the negativity out of my head.

> The one thing that did help was the boating holidays.

> One holiday on the Thames when we had mother-in-law with us, I went shopping. When I got back she was talking to a gentlemen who lived on a boat not a static house boat—a small **cruiser**. That give me an idea; the seed was sown.

> On another boating holiday, I found a book called: –'Canals Are My Home'. That gave me something to work on.

> I relied more and more on my daughter; to a large extent our roles were becoming reversed.

Some days I still had a few fragment of earlier memories:

> Best treat as a small child—going for a trip on the Thames Steamer

> Helping with a lock when I could hardly reach the balance beam. Sharing an airbed on the mill stream at Welvercote.

> Seeing a narrow boat pulling coal boats on the Oxford Canal.

> Dad trying out his new reading teaching techniques on me.

> Not being allowed to have a fairy cycle.

> The one time I went for a walk with Dad, I ripped my knee open on some barbed wire.

CHAPTER 4

Life Fell Off a Cliff

As usual, Alan had set off for work at about 5 p.m. I went to bed at the normal time, and sleeping had been better since Alan had been on nights. I do not know what time my daughter came into my room and said, "There is a policeman at the door, so you had better come down."

I blundered downstairs, and the policeman was saying something about I had better come with him, as my husband was in the hospital. Not really knowing what was happening, the two of us went with the policeman.

It transpired that while Alan had been cycling to work, he had been hit by a car. By the time we arrived at the hospital, he had been transferred from the A and E to intensive care. He was surrounded by a frightening array of tubes and machines. After a while, we found a room to rest in. After I instructed the staff to call me if there was any change, I tried to get some rest. The next couple of days were just a haze of trying to make sense of what was happening.

I could not cope with sitting in the ward with Alan. I could not communicate; he could not respond. I was terrified by all the apparatuses. When I was not dashing about, I was sitting in the anteroom next to the ward. Suddenly, some time on that Friday, I had an overwhelming sense that I should be with Alan. I sat by him and held his hand. In effect, I said good-bye.

The next day, the doctor told me his brain was no longer alive, so he asked for my permission for the machines to be switched off. At that point I was so numb, I was operating on auto-pilot.

When I realized what was happening, I just felt as though I had fallen off a cliff. All I could say was, "What will happen to me now?"

CHAPTER 5

Picking Up the Pieces

For weeks, my life was just a haze of getting through the days and arranging all the things that needed to be arranged. With help, both practical and supportive, from my church friends I got through. Gradually, I began to work through what I had lost and what I had been left to me. The thought that I had lost my dream of living on a boat seemed to confirm that my world had ended.

One day a friend said, "I know a lady who lives on a boat on her own. Would you like me to arrange for you to meet her?" At the time, that was more than I could handle, but it was a ray of hope.

I worked on through the stages of grief. Later, a friend lent me a book about grief; I was amazed to find it accurately described what I had been through. I was also amazed that I responded to a situation as others did.

When I was beginning to handle life again, just a bit, I followed up on my friend's idea. Arrangements were made, and I got myself over to Aylesbury to meet the lady on the boat. She was a friendly, helpful lady. She still worked, so she did not cruise much. But at least she lived on a boat, and she inspired me to find out more.

Though there were many things that still needed to be done, I was reading Waterways World magazine and contacting various people about boats, including the RBOA (Residential Boat Owners Association). The whole idea was building momentum. It was my son who said, "Don't you think you ought to find out if you can handle a boat on your own before you go buying one?" So I rang a hire boat company in Reading. They were not very happy about the idea, but they agreed to me hiring a small canal boat for a weekend.

It was a real adventure, my first try at single-handing, as it is called. It was a nice little boat, about twenty feet long. As you came in through the rear door, there was a little wash room and the toilet. Then the main cabin, with a table and benches, which converted to a bed at night. Ahead of that was the kitchen (or galley). With all my things loaded on board it was time to try it out. The boatyard folk advised me that the canal would be too hard for me on my own, so I pulled out onto the River Thames. There was not time to go far, so I only went round the corner and tied up between two trees. The hardest thing about single-handing is mooring up, because you need to be at both ends at once. So having tied the front mooring rope around one tree and the stern rope around another tree, I felt very pleased with myself. Then I went in and got some dinner.

The next day, I continued up the Thames. The lock keepers were very helpful and being a small boat, I was able to manage the ropes. (On the Thames, boats have to be held with a rope at each end.) I made it as far as Goring. Then I returned to Reading. All had gone very well. I think the boatyard manager was very relieved to see me back with the boat in one piece.

CHAPTER 6

Starting on the Square Hole

By the time the compensation money from Alan's accident came through, over two years later, I had chosen a boat and helped my daughter to buy a flat. There was a member at church who was a house-letting agent. I was arranging with him to let the house as a shared occupancy with my son as one of the tenants, as he was not interested in a mortgage yet.

I was going through a lot of doubt and conflict, as a number of the members and most of the elders at church were against me moving onto the boat. Yet, I felt it was something I needed to do, if only to get it out of my system. Twice before, I had chickened out of following a dream and I had always regretted it. I did not want to add a third regret.

I bought the boat. The first thing I did was to go up for a weekend on my own, to make sure I could manage it. It was a beautiful boat. It had the main cabin at the front, which was open plan for loose furniture, a kitchen with a sink, cooker, and a water heater. Then, a dinette (which is a fixed table and benches that convert to a bed at night). Then, a nice little wash room, with toilet, wash basin, and shower. The diesel engine was a converted tractor engine. Then, the special attraction of this boat for me was the rear cabin, which was a reproduction of the living quarters of the boatman's families in the working boat days, commonly called a "boatman's cabin".

The main difference in handling this boat to the one in Reading was it was sixty feet long and very much heavier. But it was a lovely boat to handle. This was my first try at single-handing in a canal lock. At home, I had worked on the theory. Now I put it into practice, one step at a time. To my relief, the weekend was a great success.

Next, my children and I took our holidays from work to fetch the boat from the Midlands. The nearest mooring, I could get was at Slough.

Time went by and I was getting worse. I decided I must go for it. I fetched the boat, with help of the family, up onto the Thames and started moving my things onto it.

Downsizing from a house to a boat was a challenge. Thank goodness for charity shops and recycling bins. I was struggling with getting the house straight; I had never really managed that in the past, and I thought the house would win again. But this time, with some help from a work mate's husband (who was a painter and decorator), I won.

The house was finished. What I decided I would need was on the boat and the house was handed over to the letting agent. The boat was my home now.

During the time I had been on the Thames, I had been calling once a week at a small local boatyard for services. They offered me a temporary mooring in their dock, so I took it. I was there for about a year.

I was still working at this time, so I commuted to work by road each day.

I was searching for what I should be doing with the boat. My original idea was that I would be traveling, not just staying in one place and using the boat like a house on water. I felt that God had allowed me to have the boat, so I wanted to use it for Him.

I found an advert about Christian retreats on boats, which I answered. I went up to the Midlands to meet the folks. It was not really what I was looking for, but I was keen to get moving.

If I was going to trust God, I would have to step out in faith. The church folks advised against it, but as they were against the boat anyway, I took no notice. But this time, perhaps I should have listened. The venture was a disaster. The retreat never materialized, the folks involved fell out, and the whole thing fell apart. But I had left work and made the first step.

I finished up on a mooring in the Midlands. I was unsure how to cope on my own. The boatyard manager said, "There's a man here on one of the boats that likes tinkering about on boats. He'll be pleased to have another one to help on." I thought, I will believe that when I see it. But to my surprise, I soon had a list of things he was doing for me on the boat.

At this time, my new friend, Rex, was living on his boat with a cousin. I soon became quite friendly with her. She renewed my interest in cross-stitch, and we often worked cross-stitch together on their boat. But she became jealous of the amount of time Rex spent on my boat.

In the end, it finished in a big bust-up.

I think there had been trouble simmering between them for a long time; the incident with me just brought things to a head. A while later, she left.

By then, I was in a real state again. I finished up back down at my daughter's again. But this time, it was more than she could handle and she sent for the doctor, who referred me to the CPN (community psychiatric nurse). She had been helpful before, but this time she said I would have to see her boss. I was referred to the consultant.

CHAPTER 7

The Secret Life of Zona

The next period is very hard to relate. It did not seem as though it was I who was in control anymore. A new person seemed to be taking over. I called that alter ego Zona.

At first, I could still make decisions for myself when I put my mind to it. But that became harder and harder. I must have been becoming more and more irrational as I finished up in the psychiatric ward of the hospital. More and more, Zona was taking over. She had her own agenda. At one stage, the doctors decided I was well enough to go to what they called a "halfway house" to get me ready for going home.

It was a nightmare, and Zona took over completely. Her only aim was to destroy me. She became obsessed with finding a way to achieve that. She was very devious. She managed to convince the doctors that I was getting better. I was given permission to have a short break. She made elaborate plans to get me out of sight long enough by hiring a caravan and also plans to get adequate medication on the way there. All to achieve her aim.

Installed in the caravan, the little me deep down inside was losing the battle. I just cried out to God for help and to forgive me for what was happening. But I felt at the time that Zona was stronger and so I took a handful of the medication. That should have been the end of me. But God intervened, and when the cleaners came to clean the caravan on change-over day, I was still alive.

An ambulance was called, and I was taken to the local hospital.

CHAPTER 8

Life Restarted

It was summer 2003, and I was still struggling. I was back on my boat, moored next to Rex. He was chaffing at the bit to get away.

When I ran out of excuses, we set out for a few weeks. Early in September, we were on our way back. I was a bit better, but not much. We met a Yorkshire couple who were new to boating. They asked us to come to Boston with them, as they needed Rex's expertise. At first we said no. But we talked it over. We had nothing particular to be back for, so we caught up with them and went to Boston.

It took about a fortnight. During that time, God healed me. Zona was gone. I could not wait to get back to base and get my life in order. It took me all the winter to get things sorted out.

I joined the choir at the church where Rex played the organ. I joined a walking group. I decided that if I was going to be part of the twenty-first century, I might as well do it properly. I had the electrics on the boat upgraded so that I could use the mains and bought a laptop computer. I then found a course to learn how to use it.

The following summer, we went away on my boat. I thought life was sorted. It was settling into a pattern, away on one or other of the boats during the summers and being involved in things on land during the winters.

In the summer of 2005, we went away on my boat as Rex was having some trouble with his boat. He had been very stressed about his boat, but I thought getting away on the boat would do the trick. At first, it seemed to. He calmed down and seemed to be enjoying himself. Then one night, for seemingly no reason, he flew into a temper. Everything I said only seemed to make it worse. I had seen him in a temper before, but nothing like this. I was worried he would give himself a heart attack or something. He said, "If you say another word I will get Russell to fetch me home." (Russell is his son.) I just stared at him, but he rang Russell anyway. Rex busied himself packing until Russell came. I begged Russell not to take him, but he said "I'm not getting involved. If he wants to come back, I'll bring him back."

When they had gone, I was just stunned.

Next morning, I was mad. Rex had left me stranded on the towpath, at least two days and a lot of large locks from home base (most of which were too big and heavy for me to manage on my own).

During my time at Langley Mill, I had joined a group called the BCF (Boaters' Christian Fellowship). Now I got the members' directory and started ringing members to see if anyone could help me move the boat. My daughter came at the weekend to help me move it to the mooring belonging to one of the members.

I thought when Rex calmed down he would ring to make up, but he didn't. My daughter persuaded me to ring him. But he said he didn't think I should come back as he didn't think it would work out.

I was not going to be moored where I was not welcome, so I started ringing around the country looking for another mooring. They are as rare as hen's teeth. Always they were suspicious that I was a live-aboard (most boatyards and marinas were not prepared to take boaters that live on their boats). I had quite a patter to get around that one. Some put me on their waiting list, some did not.

I asked myself, why should I miss out because of Rex's behaviour? I had not found a mooring to go to but I continued with my summer trip.

At least I was making more progress with the folks from the B.C.F. The first member who came to help was a young man who worked on the railways. He worked on signal maintenance, so he mostly worked at the weekends. During the week, we would travel on, then at the weekends I would moor up and he would go off to work.

This was the way I had wanted to work the boat. The trip was going well. It took us up the Trent and Mersey Canal, then down the Staffordshire and Worcestershire Canal (commonly known as the Staffs and Worcester) which brought us to Stourport-on-Severn at the junction with the River Severn. Just before the lock that lowered us into the basin, there was a beautiful little bungalow for sale. It was lunch time, so we moored in the basin. After lunch, we went back and had a look at the bungalow. I fell in love with it.

A few more phone calls and I found myself putting my house on the market and starting the process of buying the bungalow. At this point, all the transactions could be done on the phone, so we continued with the trip. My young friend came with me as far as Upton-on-Severn.

From then on, another BCF member came. We continued down the River Severn as far as the junction with the River Avon. Things with the houses were progressing. I needed an address, but I could not get a mooring.

My young railway friend came up trumps again. On his travels, he came across a new marina that had just opened. I managed to convince them that it was a temporary measure between the selling and buying of properties. So we were heading for Napton in Oxfordshire, which was just as well, as it was exciting at first not knowing where I was going. But after a while, this got to be a strain.

We headed up the Stratford Canal to Kingswood Junction and turned right, which is a little link canal, then onto the Grand Union Canal. Down the Hatton Flight to Napton Junction and straight across into the new Wigrams Turn Marina.

My friend went home, and I sorted out for my post to come to the post office in the village. I stayed there for the rest of the summer.

Any major repairs to locks and other structures that will require the closure of a waterway the British Waterways do during the winter. So that I would not be trapped at Napton for the winter, I set out for Stourport.

My BCF friend came to help and we set out. Things at Marlow were not going according to plan. The house was now single occupancy, my son having got himself a place of his own. Though the tenant was prepared to move out, she had decided to use this situation to get a council place. Though the council are now obliged to provide a place because she was being evicted and she had a child, they were being, jobs worth, and making it go through the courts.

We travelled up the North Oxford Canal to the junction near Coventry, down the Coventry Canal to the junction with the Trent and Mersey, as far as the junction at Great Haywood. Then down the Staffs and Worcester, back towards Stourport.

One evening, the lady who was selling the bungalow rang, chasing the completion date, saying she would lose the place she was after. I explained the situation I was in and managed to convince her she would not sell any quicker by starting again. It was a very traumatic phone call. I was not sure if I would lose that lovely little place at Stourport I had set my heart on.

We continued down the Staffs and Worcester until we got to Stourport. The council were still making things difficult, so it was a case of sit it out and hope for the best, which is always the most stressful part of any transaction.

When we arrived at Stourport, the wait was still going on. I arranged for my post to go to my friend's house and went to see the British Waterways about a mooring. I did not manage to get a mooring anywhere and I finished up on a temporary mooring on the towpath, which meant I had no access to services. I had a twelve-foot lock between me and a water supply and most of the winter no access to a reliable diesel supply. With the only means of electricity being running the engine, I had to keep its use to an absolute minimum. I could get to shops for food and coal, but I had to rely on candles for lighting and went once a fortnight to fill the water tank. It was a grim winter. During that time, Rex started ringing to say how lonely he was and how much he missed me.

In the spring, the sale went through at last. I started making arrangements to move into the bungalow. I had very little furniture left, so I had to start nearly from scratch.

I had decided that if I wanted to have the bungalow and the boat, I would have to have a lodger to help with the cost. Rex was still ringing incessantly and one day I let that slip on the phone. He reckoned he wanted to be the lodger. I decided 'better the devil you know' and to 'let bygones be bygones' and he moved down to Stourport. He was having a job settling, but in due course he fetched his boat down and I thought that would help.

In September that year, my daughter was to be married, so there was lots to do for the wedding. I did manage to get a short trip on the boat and everything seemed fine. It was my daughter who had troubles. Her partner's job had been relocated and they were having difficulties moving house. They borrowed the boat and moored it nearer to where he was now working, so that he did not have to travel backwards and forwards every day and my daughter transferred to the local branch of her work.

Then, soon after the wedding, Rex decided he was not settling in very well (though he seemed to me to be making friends better than I was). Then, one morning up and left on his boat and singlehanded it all the way back to Langley Mill. I was devastated.

Before long, Rex started ringing again. I would not answer the phone when it was him calling. I would not speak to him for weeks. I contacted Holiday Fellowship and booked a course in February called. 'Happily Inspired' that I hoped would cheer me up.

Christmas came and went. My daughter and son-in-law were still on the boat and there did not seem much signs that they would be off by the summer. I decided that continuing to ignore Rex was cutting off my nose to spite my face. So I contacted him. We arranged to spend the summer on his boat.

February came and I went on the course. It was all I had hoped for, and in a most beautiful setting. While chatting with the tutor on a coffee break, I discovered she was moving on to a job in Kidderminster and was looking for lodgings in that area. I explained I was in the process of sorting my place in Stourport out to let. (Kidderminster is five miles from Stourport.) We arranged for her to come and see if it would be suitable. She was happy with things as they were, which was a great relief, as I did not really know how life was going to work out.

A date was arranged, but I was not really ready, mentally or materially. When she moved in, in April, much of my stuff was still around the place, and at that point I reckoned I was coming back in September, and we were to be sharing the bungalow.

During the summer, I realized I wanted to be back on the boat and that I wanted to live on it for as long as I could manage it.

One of the houses my daughter looked at was in a village called Hopwas. As I was checking the village out for her, I reckoned it would also be a suitable spot for me. It dawned on me that even if she did not get that place, I could be there anyway, as the Coventry Canal runs through the village.

By late August, we were back on Rex's home mooring at Langley Mill, but my daughter was still on my boat. By the end of September, I was getting impatient. By October, she agreed to leave the boat. I had decided to try a towpath mooring again. I reckoned that if I planned it properly, it might work. I booked a temporary mooring through British Waterways on the visitors' mooring at Hopwas. My daughter handed the boat over at the beginning of November. I spent the winter getting the boat back the way I wanted it and preparing for the summer.

Living moored on the towpath was a challenge, but when I got into the routine of it, it worked quite well.

PART

CHAPTER

1

Life on a Boat

When one lives on land, one takes it for granted that, when one turns the tap on, water comes out. When you press the light switch, the light comes on. When you go to the toilet, the waste flushes away, and the post arrives through the letterbox. But when you live on a boat, you have to see to all these things yourself.

Water is stored in a tank. There are '"water points" (outside taps) at various places, at boatyards and marinas, at British Waterways Offices, and sometimes just by the side of the canal. One carries a long hosepipe on the boat, connects one end of it to the tap and the other end to a connection on the boat, then fills the tank; if one forgets, (one runs out of water).

If you have a mooring in a marina, etc., you may have a connection to the mains electricity, but otherwise the only electricity is what you generate yourself (by the engine for example) and store it in big batteries on board. When you are stationary in urban areas, this can cause trouble. Nowadays there are other alternatives, such as wind generators or generators run by petrol or diesel, and what I think is best in that kind of thing are solar panels.

There are two main ways of dealing with the toilet, and my boat had one of each. One was a toilet similar to a house toilet but with a tank that had to be pumped out at a boatyard, for example, and the other was like a little commode with a little tank that had to be emptied by carrying it to a receptacle.

The cooking on my boat was by bottled gas. The gas bottles had to be changed at the boatyards, etc., and as with the water, if you forgot, you ran out. My water heating was quite unusual. If the engine was running, water could be heated by that, if the central heating was on, it could be heated by that, and if neither was on, I had a gas water heater. The heating was either solid fuel or gas central heating (it took me years to get all that set up).

The post was a bigger problem, since I didn't have a fixed address. If you have a permanent mooring in a boatyard, etc., you use their address, but you have no access to your post while you are away. Otherwise, you have to get someone to take your post.

That was until a company called 'Ship to Shore' came into being. I could then use their address, and my post went to them. Each time I stopped, while I was away, I would go to the local post office and arrange an accommodation address with them, then contact Ship to Shore and they would forward any post.

Inspite of all that, I think life on a boat is well worth it.

CHAPTER 2

Life as I Intended It to Be

I did not yet feel confident enough to tackle the winter with no mooring at all.

So I booked a winter mooring with British Waterways. That is just one of the summer visitors' mooring that is rented out for the winter, November to the end of March. But there are no services so I still had to travel for water, pump-out, etc. But the mooring at Hopwas was on a long, lock-free stretch in several directions, from Streehay near the end of the Coventry Canal in one direction to Fazeley Junction in the other, and the Birmingham and Fazeley Canal from Fazeley Junction to the bottom of Curdworth Locks. So I could safely manage all that I needed on my own, Fazeley Marina on the Birmingham and Fazeley had water, diesel, pump-out, gas, rubbish disposal, and coal. The Streehay Wharf at Streehay had all these services plus a laundry facility. I arranged for the post to go to the little post office at Hopwas.

There were several moorings that were convenient for shopping. If I needed a bigger shopping centre I could get the bus from Hopwas to Tamworth or Lichfield, also from Fazeley to Birmingham. Because all the facilities were well spread out, chugging up and down kept the batteries charged up.

EXONA MOLL

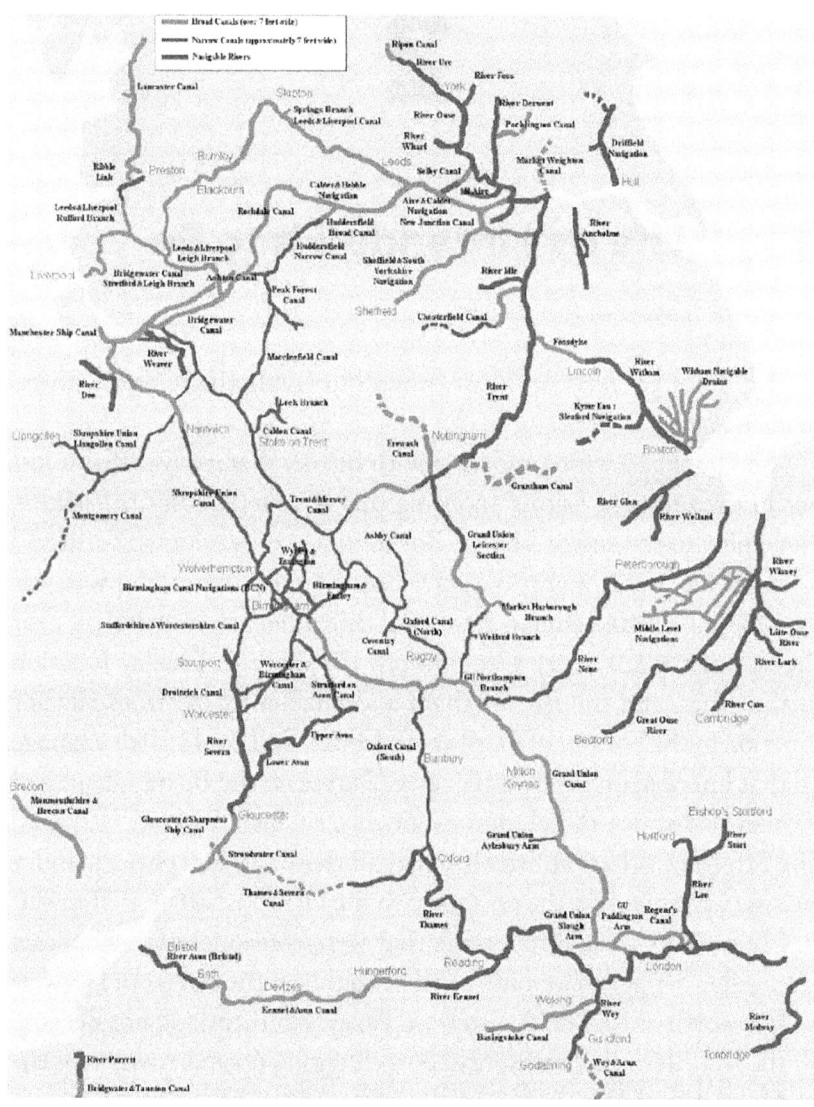

CHAPTER 3

The Winter Routine

The first job was to check the batteries. If the power was low, I would prepare to go for a run, unless the weather was so bad that I could not move, in which case I would run the engine on the spot, which is not good for it. The only two weather conditions that would prevent me from moving were a strong wind or if I was frozen in.

Where I went depended on which facilities were needed and which way I was facing. You cannot turn a sixty-foot narrow boat on the majority of the canals. There are especially wide places, called winding holes, for turning a boat around.

On days when I needed to move, I would start the engine and let it warm up while I checked whether I needed water, pump-out or shopping. Then I would plan the trip accordingly. Mostly, that first winter, I was starting out from Hopwas. If it was only water I needed and I was facing south (towards Coventry), the nearest water point was at the British Waterways Office at Fazeley.

To moor, I would pull slowly into the mooring until I was just about stopped, jump off the stern with the centre rope, anchor it temporally, then tie first the stern rope, then the front rope. The hosepipe lived on the roof. I would connect it to the water tap, flush the pipe through, then fit the other end in the tank connection. Depending how empty the tank was, filling it could take quite a long time, so I would go in and get a cup of coffee or something while I waited. Once the tank was full, I would replace the pipe, untie the ropes, always making sure the centre rope was where I could reach it, then last I would climb aboard with the centre rope.

All the procedures on a boat take a long time; it is a leisurely way of life. After the tank filled, it was usually time to make for one of the moorings sites to have lunch. If lunch was at one of the nicer sites I would probably stay to either do some jobs on the boat or some of my crafts. Later, I may decide to move to a better site for overnight or stay where I was until next day. When I needed to do the laundry, I would need to go to the boatyard at Streehay. That was quite a long run, so I would make sure I was facing the right way the night before on the home base at Hopwas. It was pretty well an all-day job to go to Streehay and do the laundry. I would wind (turn) at Streethay and moor on the towpath on the way back, usually returning to Hopwas the next day.

Another regular trip was to Fazeley Marina. That is where I usually went when the toilet needed pumping out, also to get diesel for the engine and coal. The lady in the office was very friendly and she used to have some of the cards that I made on sale for me.

If there was anything wrong with the boat, the mechanic at Debbie's Day Boats, a bit further up the Birmingham and Fazeley Canal, was usually able to help. My one main connection with life on land was the little Methodist Chapel at Hopwas. I became a regular visitor during the winter months. Also, a little later, I joined a little craft group that met in the Hopwas village hall.

Travelling for the services was usually sufficient to keep the batteries charged up, but if I needed extra power, like when I needed the computer and printer running for making the inserts for my cards, I would have to run the engine on the mooring. So I would moor out in the country that night.

CHAPTER 4

Summers As I Originally Intended

I was having better success with planning the summers, as I had originally hoped when I first moved on the boat. I had a number of friends through contacts in the Midlands and the BCF and members of my family who were keen to join me.

So the plan was for different couples to join me for a week or so at a time, to help me with the locks, etc., so that I could venture further afield, and they could have a holiday afloat. Though I enjoyed the single-handing that I'd done when I first had the boat, I was getting older, and there are some areas where that is very difficult.

I had the boat winded and facing north towards Streehay and Fradley Junction. The first couple were friends I met in the Midlands. They came to me at Hopwas, we loaded their things on board, and away we went. It was their first time on a narrow boat, and they were very excited. We set out for the junction with the Trent and Mersey Canal at Fradley, turning left towards the first lock. We moored up and I went to the lock with them to show them how to set it. Then I returned to the boat to bring it into the lock. They soon got the idea of how to work the sluices to fill the lock to bring the boat up to the next level. There was only a short distance to the next lock, so my friends walked up, and I brought the boat. There is quite a distance to the next lock, so they climbed aboard. After the third lock, there is quite a long, lock-free stretch, so they were able to have a rest.

It was all going very well, and they were really enjoying it. The Trent and Mersey is a broad-beam canal; that is, two narrow boats or one broad beam boat can fit into the locks. All the locks and the lock gates are bigger than narrow canals, so the lock gates are heavier and harder to work. Not only that, but if a narrow boat is in the lock on its own there is nothing to hold it still while the water is filling the lock, so it is quite dangerous to work on one's own.

At last, the boating was a real success. I was able to live the life I wanted and give others a good, cheap holiday.

During the day, we shared all the duties. At night, they slept in the dinette and I slept in the boatman's at the back.

We continued up the Trent and Mersey Canal as far as Haywood Junction, then turned off onto the Staffs and Worcester. That is a lovely canal. It is back to narrow locks, and it runs through very pretty countryside. My friends stayed with me until the Autherley Junction, which is the junction with the Shropshire Union Canal (affectionately known as the Shroppie). I stopped there at the Oxley Marina, where I was having some work done.

When the work was finished, one of the chaps from the BCF joined me for the next part of the trip. We set off down the Shroppie. The locks here are mostly in groups called flights; there are three flights with long, lock-free stretches in between. We passed the junction to the Llangollen Canal. You may have heard of the famous Pontcuysyllte Aqueduct. That is on the Llangollen Canal. I had been across it on a previous occasion, but this time we were going straight on to the next junction, which is the Barbridge Junction. That took us onto the Middlewich Branch of the Shropshire Union. There are only a few odd locks until one reaches the junction at Middlewich.

This brought us back onto the Trent and Mersey and broadbeam locks. My crew stayed with me as far as Northwich, where he could get the train home. The next stretch was all lock free and I continued on my own through Anderton where the great boat lift lifts boats down to the River Weaver. I cruised through three tunnels, Barton Tunnel, Saltersford Tunnel, and the 1239-yard-long Preston Tunnel, then on further north onto the Bridgewater Canal. After about another five miles, the canal starts to go through more built-up areas, until I got to a little place called Lymm, where my daughter and son-in-law joined me for a weekend. Then, I continued alone through the outskirts of Manchester, passed Waters Meeting, which is the junction to Manchester centre, then bore left past Trafford Park and Leigh. Along this stretch, I picked up my original BCF friend. We were heading for the crossing of the River Ribble and the new stretch of canal that connected to the Lancaster Canal.

It was a tricky pick-up. There was not really anywhere to moor, so I'd had to moor farther away the night before, then when my friend's train was due I cruised slowly towards the bridge near the railway station (thank goodness for mobile phones). The pick-up went smoothly and we were away.

He was keen to do this stretch, as he had done the Ribble crossing from north to south, but not south to north, and I was glad of his experience.

We made good progress towards Wigan, which is the junction with the Leeds and Liverpool Canal. In a previous year, I had cruised the Leeds and Liverpool Canal from Wigan to Leeds while I was travelling with Rex, with the help of my son.

This time we turned left, towards Liverpool. We were back to broad-beam locks. One of the problems with cruising through urban areas is that the propeller gets more fouled with rubbish. We were coming out of one of the Wigan locks when the engine just stopped. I managed to pull over, and it was time to go down the weed hatch. This is not a nice job, as one has to reach down into the canal water, which is often so mucky one cannot see a thing. This time, it was a jacket wrapped around the propeller. I managed to get it off whole, but usually it was a case of cutting off the offending item with a knife, bit by bit.

All then went well to the junction with the Rufford Branch (which was where we were going next), but we were running ahead of time. One has to book the crossing at the River Ribble in advance. We had time to spare, so we decided to continue towards Liverpool. Gradually, the canal got in a worse and worse state. We moored up to discuss what to do. A resident from a nearby house advised us not to go much further. We thanked her and turned back at the next winding hole.

Back at the junction, we turned left onto the Rufford Branch towards the River Douglas. We stopped in Rufford instead, which was a nice stop. We arrived at Tarleton just on time. The party for the crossing all arrived at the mooring point and we were checked in by the British Waterways staff. The time for leaving the river lock was governed by the tide, as the River Douglas is tidal at that point.

When the water levels were correct, the lock keeper opened the gates and we were away. The river got wider and wider, so that by the time we got to the junction with the River Ribble it was like we were going out to sea. The whole fleet turned right, upstream towards the new Ribble Link. It was really exciting; narrow boats are not built for going out to sea. At one point, we could not see land, just what looked like sea. At last, the tiny opening came into sight. It was very important not to turn too soon; otherwise, the boat would get stuck on mud banks. It was nerve-racking to judge the right time to turn. It was a relief when we were safely into the link. The link was a little stream that had been dug out to make it navigable. It is the first totally new canal that has been dug for two hundred years.

It was very narrow and twisty in places. We made careful progress up to the locks. They are a very strange flight with an almost U-bend in the middle. This section is manned, so there are lock keepers to give instructions. Managing this with a sixty-foot boat is quite a challenge. Safely up the link onto the Lancaster Canal, we stopped for a break. Soon after that, my friend left for home.

There are no locks on the Lancaster Canal. I spent a pleasant summer cruising up and down that canal.

There were two crew members who joined me during that time. One was a BCF member. While he was with me, I took the opportunity to explore the only section in that part of the world that does have locks, the Glasson Branch, which connects the Lancaster Canal with the port at Glasson. It was a lovely trip and a strange experience being moored in the port alongside seagoing ships. We returned to the main channel and travelled as far as the canal has been restored to date. I then took him back to Lancaster to get transport home. Also, my brother joined me for a short holiday.

My favorite stop on the Lancaster was at Hest Bank, where the canal comes within walking distance of the sea, looking across Morecombe Bay.

At the end of my stay on the Lancaster, my son and daughter in-law joined me at Preston. We came back down the link. That was very strange; a sixty-foot boat is not able to take the U-bend coming back down so we had to navigate into the middle lock backwards. There was another fleet of boats to cross the Ribble. We all collected at the mooring at the bottom of the link. We had to wait for the tide to be right.

When the signal came, we all set out on the high seas again, all hoping we would find the turning into the River Douglas all right—if not, we would be in the Irish Sea. My son and daughter in-law stayed with me until Parbold, back on the Leeds and Liverpool. Then with the help of other members of the Fellowship, I made my way back down the Trent and Mersey to my winter territory.

CHAPTER 5

Winter Really Wild

Over the last year, I had developed confidence in fending for myself on the towpath. So this winter, I did not commit myself to a winter mooring. I kept on the move within the winter boundaries. There were several favourite places including the B.W. moorings at Hopwas, the towpath by the Methodist Chapel at Hopwas, the mooring at Bone Hill, the Fazeley mooring at the end of the Birmingham and Fazeley, and best of all, the towpath on the tree-lined stretch beyond Drayton Bassett, near the Kingsbury Water Park, on the way towards Birmingham. There are plenty of other between Fazeley and Streehay.

The little post office had been closed, so I had to transfer the post to the post office at Fazeley.

As before, which direction I went depended on which services or facilities I needed. This winter, I got involved in more things on land, including activities at the Anglican Church at Fazeley, including a house group on a weekday evening. I went back to the Methodists at Hopwas and the craft group at Hopwas.

The winter that year really tested my resolve, as there was a lot of frost and snow. Quite often, the canal had a coating of ice and a few times I was frozen in. Mostly when it was a frost the ice broke up as soon as boats started to move, but there was one morning when the ice was thicker than usual. Though I was on a nice mooring, there was no access to any services or a bus route, etc. I waited for some time for a boat to pass but nobody was on the move. When at last someone did get through, it did not break the ice around my boat. I managed to do it myself directly in front of the boat by hitting the ice with my pole, and I decided I would try to get to Hopwas. At least there, I could get a bus, so I could get to shops, and if the weather got too bad I could get to my daughter's.

I started off, and the ice was quite thick. It creaked and groaned as the sheets moved. I was making slow progress. Then, as I came to a more open stretch, the ice got thicker, and I ground to a halt. If there had been a crew on board, they could be at the front with the pole, breaking the ice, but on my own the steering is at the back, and it was a bit dodgy. I backed up a bit and ran at the ice. It gave way a bit. I had to keep backing up and ramming the ice for quite a way round that exposed bend. Eventually, the ice was not quite so thick, and I started making slow progress again. It took me several hours to reach the towpath behind the Methodists. It is slightly more sheltered there, so the ice was not so thick. I managed to moor up there, and I stayed put. Luckily, the frozen spell did not last too long before I was able to move again.

Another morning when the canal was frozen, I was up near Curdworth by the Kingsbury Water Park. While I was waiting for some traffic on the canal, there was a little robin hopping about in the hedge. I fetched some scraps of bread and started throwing bits on the towpath for him. He got bolder and bolder. After a while, a boat went by, and I was able to get on the move. The robin seemed quite annoyed that I was going; he wanted some more bread. The boat makes a wonderful hide for watching the wildlife; especially along that stretch, there was plenty to watch.

The following spring, there was one particular family of ducks at Hopwas. I was often in stitches watching them. The mother duck would set off and all the little ducklings would set off after her, but there was always one duckling that would not behave. He would not follow the others; when all the other ducklings got into the water to follow mum, he would play up and stay on the bank. The mother would have to turn all the well-behaved ducklings back so she could chase the maverick into the water.

Eventually, the summer came, and I was ready to start on the next adventure.

CHAPTER 6

My Second Summer

This time, I travelled south. My family helped me with the first section. I picked them up at Fazeley. They spent the weekend with me. We cruised up the Coventry Canal, up the Glascote Locks, through Polesworth, and up the Atherstone Flight. After that, there is a long, lock-free stretch, so I continued on my own through Nuneaton, to Hawkesbury Junction, and onto the North Oxford Canal, until I got to Rugby. My BCF friend joined me there. We continued upstream to Braunston Turn, where the Oxford joins the Grand Union Canal. The Oxford was built long before the Grand Union (which is the canal that runs from London to Birmingham). When they built the Grand Union, they cut across the Oxford, widening the section where the two overlap. Now the Oxford is in two halves, usually referred to as the North and the South. We cruised on to the South Oxford past the Wigrams Turn Marina, where I was moored while I was buying the bungalow at Stourport, then past the windmill at Napton, turning south again to Banbury, where my friend left me and my brother joined me.

The South Oxford winds its way south to Oxford. That was our home town. He left me there and went to visit our stepmother.

The crew that were to have joined me at Oxford could not come. But they had arranged for a young friend of theirs to come instead.

He duly arrived and we were off again, cruising down the Thames as far as Reading.

My daughter was about to have her first child. I had arranged for a mooring in a Marina at Reading so that I could return to her place to help out. I had not cancelled the trip, because three crews had booked their holidays with me, so I did not want to let them down. My grandson was born on the twenty-ninth of July. Later, I returned to Reading to continue the trip.

First, it was my son and daughter-in-law who joined me. We cruised nearly the whole length of the Kennet and Avon Canal, including the Cane Hill Flight, as far as Bath. Then down the famous Cane Hill Flight. They left me at Bath to return to work. One of the BCF members joined me for the return journey. At Reading, the crew changed again. My BCF friend wanted to do the stretch of the Thames from Reading to London. So he joined me at Reading.

We continued downstream to Marlow, where I used to live. We were moored up on the park moorings, and there was a hotel boat moored there. My friend went to talk to the owner. The boat did a trip on down the Thames from London to the flood barrier. That was another stretch he wanted to do, so he booked a trip for the next year. I was not available, but I said perhaps I could go another time. We continued down to Brantford, which is the junction with the Grand Union. We came up through the lock and moored in the basin.

I had a short break before my next crew was due. I was glad of a rest, as my right leg was giving me trouble. I could not stand for long enough to do the steering for any length of time. The next crew reckoned he could not do the steering. My daughter and son in-law, with my new grandson, were coming down to see me. So they stayed and gave me a hand. I sat with the baby, and the rest of them handled the boat.

I limped back to the Coventry Canal. I had the boat booked in at Springwood Haven, Nuneaton, to have the bottom blacked. Between us, we managed to get the boat there. I used to paint the boat myself—Rex and I had done the two boats between us—but now I had to have it done for me at the boatyard.

CHAPTER 7

A Rather Different Winter

I decided to stay on the upper level of the Coventry Canal, with my range being from the top of the Atherstone Locks to Hawkesbury Junction and also the Ashby Canal. My main boatyard for services was Springwood Haven; it had all the facilities I needed. The main shopping area was Atherstone, which had quite a good range of shops. There were a number of good mooring sites and to start with I cruised up and down as I had done the last two winters. But my leg was becoming more and more troublesome. After a while, I decided I would need to find a mooring and began ringing all the boatyards, etc., in the area.

I found a boatyard at Stoke Golding, halfway up the Ashby Canal, which would take me on a winter mooring. I set out and installed myself on my new mooring. It had water on site and an electrical hook-up but no other facilities. So, though I was able to stay put most of the time, I still had to travel to get diesel, gas, and pump-out. At first, I could manage that, but as the winter wore on, it was getting to be more of a struggle. After a few months, I realized my time on the boat was coming to an end. I had arranged that I would spend Christmas and New Year with my daughter, so I kept the festive season as arranged. In the New Year, the weather was very bad. I stayed an extra week or so until the weather improved a bit. But when I returned to the boat I realized something had to be done.

Sometime earlier, I had lost the ex-tutor as my tenant. I now let the bungalow through a letting agent on a short-term let. I contacted the agent to say I would have to give notice to reclaim the property. The required notice was given, and arrangements were made for me to return to Stourport.

As soon as the winter stoppages were over, I arranged for two friends plus my son to bring the boat from Stoke Golding to Stourport. The properties have mooring rights by the canal, but there are more properties than there are moorings, and this time the moorings were taken. I had always said that if I could not travel, I would sell the boat. So rather than try to get another mooring, which I could not really afford on just my pension, I would put the boat straight on the market.

Though I'd always known the boat would not go on forever, I had hoped it would have gone for a few more years. But I was a very different person now to what I was when I first moved onto a life afloat.

www.ingramcontent.com/pod-product-compliance
Ingram Content Group UK Ltd.
Pitfield, Milton Keynes, MK11 3LW, UK
UKHW022218230426
12048UKWH00016BA/930